D1708809

ANARCHY

Kerry Hinton

rosen publishing's
**rosen
central**®

New York

Published in 2020 by The Rosen Publishing Group, Inc.
29 East 21st Street, New York, NY 10010

Copyright © 2020 by The Rosen Publishing Group, Inc.

First Edition

Library of Congress Cataloging-in-Publication Data

Names: Hinton, Kerry, author.
Title: Anarchy / Kerry Hinton.
Description: First edition. | New York : Rosen Central, 2020. | Series: Examining political systems | Includes bibliographical references and index.
Identifiers: LCCN 2018016584| ISBN 9781508184331 (library bound) | ISBN 9781508184324 (pbk.)
Subjects: LCSH: Anarchism—History—Juvenile literature. | Anarchism—Juvenile literature.
Classification: LCC HX826 .H56 2019 | DDC 335/.8309—dc23
LC record available at https://lccn.loc.gov/2018016584

Manufactured in the United States of America

On the cover: An Occupy Wall Street protestor wears a Guy Fawkes mask (*right*); on May Day in 1970 (*upper left*), activists protested the Vietnam War. When white nationalist Richard Spencer spoke at Michigan State University in 2018, hundreds of anarchists and antifascists went to the campus to protest the event (*lower left*).

CONTENTS

INTRODUCTION

The word "anarchy" can conjure images of violence, terror, and revolution. Despite these negative representations, "anarchy" also refers to a political philosophy. Originally, "anarchy" meant "absence of a leader." The word was born in Ancient Greece and combines "an–," which means "without," and *archos*, which means "ruler." In the nineteenth century, this more accurate definition helped launch the social movement known as anarchism. Anarchism has often been misunderstood. Even some self-proclaimed anarchists do not understand the intentions behind anarchist theory. Social media is full of posts and links containing misleading or incorrect information about anarchism. Many politicians and philosophers often believe that the goals of anarchism are nothing more than wishful thinking done by dreamers.

What are those goals? In the words of minister and author Lyman Abbott (1835–1922), "Anarchism … rests upon the doctrine that no man has a right to control by force the action of any other man." Simply put, anarchism is about the personal freedom to live as one pleases, wherever one pleases. Modern anarchists are against laws and ideas that obstruct freedom such as racism, fascism, and capitalism. For anarchists, most unjust and oppressive aspects of society are caused or made worse by a state or government; one example of government's failure is in the large divides between the wealthy and the poor. There are many different strains of anarchist theory, and each one has differing ideas on an acceptable

The antifascist movements of the twentieth and twenty-first centuries have often drawn support from the anarchist community. Both groups agree that racism and fascism prevent people from living truly free lives.

amount of government. Some want complete and total freedom from the state, while others want limitations on it. Many anarchic goals are not wild political beliefs from society's fringe. On both the left (more liberal) and right (more conservative), people have embraced and included anarchist ideas in their politics. For example, socialist Libertarians may not want to abolish government altogether, but they want to make it as small as possible to increase personal freedom. The concept of reducing "big government" is a feature of other political parties also.

Anarchists argue that order and community can exist without a hierarchy, but how to remove that hierarchy has always been a divisive issue. Some anarchist theories embrace using violence to create social change, a strategy that has ended up hurting their causes. Violent acts were common in the first few decades of the twentieth century and turned public opinion against anarchist goals and methods. As the Cold War between Russia and the United States escalated after World War II, attention began to turn from anarchism to Communism. In the twenty-first century, interest in anarchy has begun to increase once more. People around the world are exploring it as an alternative to the problems of wage inequality, poverty, and hatred.

HOW WE GOVERN

T he government of a society determines how that society interacts with its citizens and other nations. In order to discuss the idea of a leaderless government, an examination of how governments with leaders function may be helpful. One of the first philosophers to explore the concepts behind governments was Aristotle.

ARISTOTLE

Aristotle (384–322 BCE) was a Greek philosopher and teacher. Along with his groundbreaking work in philosophy, biology, and psychology, his writings also form the basis of modern political science. Aristotle used a series of classifications to examine how a state or government could

In addition to establishing the foundations of political science, Aristotle also contributed to the development of zoology, geology, and anatomy.

be built and maintained. For Aristotle, a government's type was determined by: (1) the number of people who had power and (2) the goals those people had for their societies. Without care and attention, these systems were more likely to fail. Their success was also determined by ethics—the rules societies use to choose between right and wrong. Unethical behavior and the abuse of power would raise the possibility that a government could become corrupted. Aristotle proposed three types:

MONARCHY: RULE BY ONE

A monarchy exists when a country is ruled by a king or queen, and leadership is passed down to a child or younger relative. Within these governments, rulers have control over all decisions on the welfare of a nation. If power is abused, a monarchy can become a tyranny, or absolute monarchy. Such an oppressive government can sometimes use violence and ignore the law to oppress citizens.

ARISTOCRACY: RULE BY THE FEW

In an aristocracy, leadership is determined by wealth and social status. Like the rulers of monarchies, aristocrats' power and control are often transferred through birth. At its best, an aristocracy makes decisions that benefit all citizens, but selfish behavior could create an oligarchy. Like a monarchy, an oligarchy has the potential to fail if the self-interest of the ruling class overtakes the needs of the rest of society.

POLITY: RULE BY MANY

A polity is a nation or state that has a government with laws and an arranged structure. In Aristotle's view, when a polity

SOCRATES, PLATO, AND ARISTOTLE

Philosophers build on the works of their predecessors in an effort to reach new truths. Aristotle didn't develop his philosophies on his own—he relied on lessons from his teachers to develop his own political theories. He was fortunate to have some of the greatest minds the world has ever known to guide him: Socrates and Plato.

Socrates (469–399 BCE) was one of the founders of Western philosophy whose work had a tremendous influence on modern Europe, Russia, and parts of the Middle East. Socrates is best known for the creation of the Socratic method to use logic and reasoning to arrive at conclusions.

Socrates' most famous and influential student was Plato (427–347 BCE). Plato's curiosity led him to explore and write about theology, language, and political philosophy. In the *Republic*, Plato explored the idea of just and fair government. Aside from his philosophical writings, Plato also founded the Academy in Athens, the world's first university. Subjects included biology, astronomy, and mathematics. During this time, Plato met Aristotle, who became one of his best students. After graduating, Aristotle used the collective knowledge of Socrates and Plato to explore new philosophical territory. This trio's combined writings and work played a large role in the development of Western philosophy.

became corrupt it became a democracy, which at the time meant majority rule. This definition is much different from the way modern democracies are usually described. To Aristotle, the majority was incapable of making decisions that would benefit an entire society. The result would be a descent into disorganized mob rule.

Aristotle believed systems that operated for the common good were the best types of government. He also believed that these types of rule operated in cycles; for example, a monarchy that slips into tyranny would ultimately become a democracy. The negative outcomes associated with each type contributed to the development of anarchist philosophy two thousand years later.

MODERN GOVERNMENT

During the nineteenth century, philosophers and political scientists realized that Aristotle's classifications were incomplete. Some of the governing models of the nineteenth century had not even

This fourteenth-century drawing shows men at arms and men who advise from Aristotle's *Politics*. *Politics* is an eight-volume work that discusses the best aspects of a just and ethical society that benefits all citizens.

existed when Aristotle wrote *Politics*. These newer classifications differ slightly depending on the theorist, but most include the following types:

DEMOCRACY

A democracy is a government that obeys the laws of a constitution. It involves the general public who vote for people to represent them in the making of laws and management of their state, province, or country. Democracies can vary in their structures from country to country. For example, the United States is a presidential democracy, while Australia is a parliamentary government.

COMMUNISM

A Communist government is ruled by one permanent party that represents the proletariat, or working class. There is no individual ownership in these regimes—all land, goods, and the equipment used to produce them are owned by the state. The state also controls the national economy. Aside from Cuba, North Korea, and the People's Republic of China, there are very few Communist governments in the world today.

DICTATORSHIP

Dictatorships are also known as totalitarian regimes. In dictatorships, leaders have ultimate power and citizens are expected to obey every rule or suffer the consequences. In many cases, there are few elected representatives. These oppressive governments can be controlled by civilian, military, or religious leaders. The ancient Roman republic employed dictators during rebellions to unify the government, but only for a limited time.

Dictators, or despots, usually stay in power permanently unless they are overthrown or removed from office.

MONARCHY

Most monarchies today are much different from those of the past. Most countries with a king or queen today leave the task of government to an elected parliament. For example, the United Kingdom is a constitutional monarchy with a separate political branch that is responsible for lawmaking and governing.

FEDERAL SYSTEMS

Large nations such as the United States and Canada employ federal systems to govern. These structures are made up of smaller provinces or states. No one division is more powerful than the larger organization, but each one has its own smaller government that is allowed to govern its citizens. The governing of federal systems can look very different from country to country. The United States operates as a constitutional democracy. China uses some aspects of a federal system by having several branches of government (legislative, executive, judicial, and military) even though they are a one-party state.

CHAPTER 2

THE DAWN OF ANARCHISM

Anarchism grew out of socialism, a political and economic movement that began in Europe in the eighteenth and nineteenth centuries. Its popularity was boosted by two major changes in society: the Enlightenment and the Industrial Revolution.

ENLIGHTENMENT AND INDUSTRY

During the Age of Enlightenment (1685–1815), Europe experienced incredible advances in science, mathematics, politics, and philosophy. Intellectuals believed that humans could use logic and reason to make decisions that would benefit society as a whole, not just a select few. Intellectuals opposed the aristocracy, monarchies, and the Catholic Church. The concepts of personal liberty, religious tolerance, and representative government became important. For the thinkers of the Enlightenment, society needed to consider human needs and well-being above profit in order to allow people to live moral lives. These ideals had a worldwide effect. They helped inspire the American and French political revolutions of the late

The execution of King Louis XVI in 1793 marked the beginning of the Reign of Terror, a yearlong series of arrests and executions of citizens who were not loyal to the revolution. In the following year, more than fifteen thousand "enemies of the state" were beheaded.

eighteenth century. "Liberty, equality, and fraternity!" became a common cry during the French Revolution.

Enlightenment ideas were at odds with the capitalist system that drove the technological advances of the time. In a capitalist society, the means of production were owned by companies or individuals. These "means" include anything that is used to make things, including land, factories, and equipment. The Industrial Revolution, which began in Britain in 1760, allowed

EFFECTS OF THE INDUSTRIAL REVOLUTION

The life of the working class during the Industrial Revolution was harsh. By the mid-1800s, the Industrial Revolution had spread throughout Europe and America. Machines could now perform tasks more quickly than humans. Agriculture was no longer the focus of people's everyday life. Many small farmers lost their jobs through advances in technology. This job loss caused a shift from rural life to a more urban existence since people had to move to work at these new jobs.

Larger urban populations created a new set of problems. Businesses exploited workers, paying them the smallest wages possible. Employees often worked six or seven days a week, sometimes earning pennies per hour. Factories and mills often employed children and paid them even less. As electricity, the gas engine, and steel were invented, conditions became even worse. Pollution increased and worsened worker health.

In short, workers during the Industrial Revolution had no real protection, and this lack led to the formation of labor unions to advocate for workers. The appeal of anarchist theories eventually drew many workers to embrace anarchism as a path to a life of fairness and dignity.

the manufacture of goods at a larger scale than ever. Increased production required more labor. Before this time, most people made their own goods or bought them from craftspeople who ran small businesses. Mass manufacturing eliminated many people's professions and forced them to find work in larger industries. As more people lost ownership of the tools of production, the financial gap between owners and workers widened. Replacing capitalism became a driving force of this new socialist theory.

Many agreed that change was needed, but debated on how to achieve it. Social reformers thought that these systems could be reformed, while others felt that capitalism should be destroyed for real change to occur. Some of these thinkers were the earliest contributors to modern anarchism.

THINKING ABOUT ANARCHISM

By the mid-eighteenth century, the world was becoming more mechanized and violent, and many thinkers did not believe that reason alone could solve modern society's problems. This belief would be central to both Communist and anarchist theories.

JEAN-JACQUES ROUSSEAU (1712–1778)

Jean-Jacques Rousseau, a French philosopher born in Switzerland, believed that human beings were similar to animals. What makes us different, he argued, is "perfectibility," the ability to learn and improve our situations. However, Rousseau placed limits on this progress. He believed mankind had strayed

In addition to his philosophical writings, Jean-Jacques Rousseau also had a talent for musical composition. A song from one of his operas was used as the basis of a piece by Ludwig van Beethoven.

Like Aristotle, Immanuel Kant was interested in the application of ethics in everyday life. Many of these views are contained in his masterwork entitled *A Critique of Pure Reason* (1781).

too far from primitive societies. As he states in *Discourse on the Origin of Inequality* (1754), "Man is born pure, it is society that corrupts."

Rousseau also disliked private property. He believed the desire to gain raw materials from land would make men greedy and lead to control of the poorer classes. Rousseau struggled to find a balance between the individual and society; to him, people were meant to work together, not alone. As he says in *The Social Contract* (1762), "Man is born free, but everywhere he is in chains."

Rousseau also discusses the "general will," the idea that people should decide together what is best for a society. Rousseau believed that by giving up a small amount of freedom, citizens could contribute to the common good, creating freedom within the system.

IMMANUEL KANT (1724–1804)

Immanuel Kant was the most influential German philosopher of the Enlightenment. He was interested in patterns of human activity. To Kant, societies developed depending on how they viewed the relationship among force, freedom, and law. He outlines the possibilities in *Anthropology from a Pragmatic Point of View* (1798):

   A. Law and freedom without force (anarchy)
   B. Law and force without freedom (despotism)
   C. Force without freedom and law (barbarism)
   D. Force with freedom and law (republic)

Like Rousseau, Kant thought that a society was not always an obstacle to freedom. He also supported the social contract and general will, but believed that the state had the responsibility to make sure that freedom was equal for all.

WILLIAM GODWIN (1756–1836)

William Godwin was a British philosopher whose work formed the basis of philosophical anarchism. In his most famous work, *An Inquiry Concerning Political Justice* (1793), he argues that all forms of government are corrupt and will eventually be replaced. Newer systems, he said, would be driven by a "personal morality" that would develop as mankind's accumulated knowledge increased.

Godwin also believed in utilitarianism, a philosophy that says the best and most just decisions are those that consider the effect they have on everyone. Godwin envisioned a time when only individual morality would guide citizens, but he was against using violence to improve society. Godwin's beliefs marked the birth of modern anarchism. His successors would use these ideas to further develop the philosophy.

PIERRE-JOSEPH PROUDHON (1809–1865)

A French philosopher, Pierre-Joseph Proudhon was the first person to openly identify as an anarchist. Prior to this point, the word was considered an insult. While socialists thought that change should come gradually, anarchists supported immediate and total change. Without immediate and total change, they argued, those in power would refuse to allow a new system to replace the old one. Like many writers of the era, Proudhon was concerned with the dangers of private property gained without labor. In *What Is Property? Or, an Inquiry into the Principle of Right and of Government* (1840), he wrote "Property is theft!"

Proudhon thought the majority of a society would suffer if property was owned by a government or a select few. In his mind, no one could claim sole ownership of raw materials. He also opposed wage labor since it took goods from the people who made them. Proudhon believed in spontaneous order, the idea that a society could organize without any leaders. Spontaneous order lay at the center of a new system he called mutualism. In a mutualist system, the means of production would be controlled equally by the workers. Banks would charge very little interest and be owned by the public as well. People from all levels of society would be equally able to trade for things they needed. They could conduct this trading individually or as members of cooperatives—groups that organized voluntarily to exchange goods. Proudhon thought this type of society could end war, dictatorships, and forced labor.

CHAPTER 3

ANARCHISM GROWS UP

Proudhon's theories of mutualism were only the beginning of anarchist thought. Writers and thinkers continued to build on his ideas. While they shared some core beliefs, socialists and anarchists had many different viewpoints. While Proudhon was in Paris in the 1840s, he met a fellow philosopher with his own ideas about reforming society: Karl Marx.

KARL MARX (1818–1883)

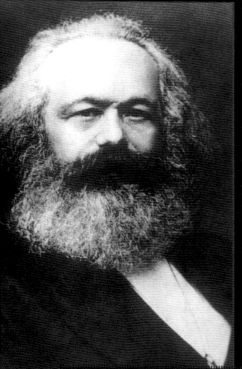

Karl Marx was a German philosopher and revolutionary socialist. He shared Rousseau's view that taking the general will of a society into account ensured equality. Marx also believed that a return to some of the

Karl Marx's writings had an enormous impact on the development of social science, which examines the relationship between individuals and the larger society.

ideals of primitive societies could improve modern life. Like many, Marx was bothered by the gap in wealth between owners and workers. Marx's solution to these problems was Communism. In 1848, he cowrote *The Communist Manifesto* with Friedrich Engels (1820–1895). The Manifesto traces the progression of societies from the feudal systems of the Middle Ages to capitalism. It concludes that all cultures involve a struggle between two groups: the bourgeoisie, who controlled land and capital, and the proletariat, who supplied the labor. Marx believed the proletariat would eventually revolt against the upper classes to destroy capitalism. Land and resources would be shared equally and the concepts of money and social class would be eliminated. Universal education would help make social classes and the state unnecessary. The pamphlet ends with the words: "Workingmen of all countries, unite."

MAX STIRNER (1806–1856)

While many anarchists could agree with socialists on goals but not methods, some refused. The German philosopher Max Stirner theorized a new form of anarchism known as egoist anarchism. It focused on self-interest, since most aspects of society were designed to oppress people. In *The Ego and Its Own: The Case of the Individual Against Authority* (1844), he states that all religions, governments, and state institutions are meaningless ghosts or "spooks." All of these, he believed, demanded control over the individual. Stirner also spoke out against higher education; to him, education should be tailored to help each person become truly individual. Stirner believed that every human being is unique, and any effort to change or reduce that uniqueness would hold that person back. This work signaled the birth of individualist anarchism. For egoists and existentialists, conformity was damaging to the human spirit's need for freedom.

MIKHAIL BAKUNIN (1814–1876)

Bakunin's path to anarchy ran through the military. As an officer in the Russian army, he served his country on the border of Poland. After realizing that the Russian Empire was occupying and oppressing Poland, he resigned his commission and left the military. For Bakunin, personal freedom meant very little without embracing the concepts of community and (social) equality. Bakunin shared William Godwin's view that government would always become corrupted.

After Bakunin moved to Paris in the 1840s, he met many socialist thinkers, including Proudhon and Karl Marx. As his

Many Russian collective farms, or *kolkhoz*, were owned by the state. Each combined the labor of up to three hundred families to grow crops that were used as payment to the state.

theories became more radical, he proposed the complete removal of the state, money, and private property. Bakunin envisioned that there would be no hierarchy, but a direct democracy where people would make decisions together. He called the system collective anarchism, or collectivism. Bakunin took inspiration from Proudhon, but disagreed with Proudhon's views on property ownership. Bakunin is also credited with spreading revolutionary anarchist ideals throughout Europe and Russia. Bakunin's willingness to use violence (against state institutions but not against citizens) set him apart from other anarchist philosophers of the day.

THE FIRST INTERNATIONAL, MARX, AND BAKUNIN

The International Workingmen's Association (IWA), or First International, was formed in London in 1864. The First International was the first labor union in modern history. Marx did not take part in its formation, but he was invited to be a member of its General Council. Although the First International was dedicated to worker unity, women were not allowed membership for the first year. Marx quickly became a leading voice in the organization, but other members opposed his views. Mutualist followers of Proudhon objected to Marx's communism, and tensions only rose when Bakunin joined the IWA in 1868. This led to a split between Bakunin's collectivists and Marx's supporters. Marx still believed in revolution to achieve change, but he favored a form of change that would occur legally from within the system itself. Bakunin believed revolutionary action was justifiable and necessary for change. He advocated the use of secret societies and organizations, even staring a subgroup called the Social-Democratic Alliance (SDA) within the IWA. Bakunin was expelled from the IWA in 1872.

PETER KROPOTKIN (1842–1921)

Peter Kropotkin was a disciple of Bakunin from an aristocratic Moscow family. Although he grew up in a privileged family, Kropotkin felt more connected to the servants who cared for him as a child than the members of his class. He became an officer in the Russian army after graduating from an elite military academy called the Page Corps. While stationed in Siberia, he became deeply affected by the terrible working and living conditions of the gold miners there. In a letter to his brother, he wrote, "This

is where one can gaze every day to one's heart's content on the enslavement of the worker by capital, and at the mani-festation of the great law of the reduction in reward with the increase in work."

Kropotkin began to dedicate his life to social justice. Like his countryman Bakunin, he left the military after witnessing the exploitation of workers. He then joined the Tchaikovsky Circle, a revolutionary group based in Moscow. He began writing pamphlets that brought the ideas of revolutionary anarchism to the working poor of the Russian Empire. He was imprisoned for his ideas in 1874.

As Peter Kropotkin began to age, he spoke out against the violence he supported as a young man.

After two years, Kropotkin escaped but would not return to Russia for over thirty years. While in exile, Kropotkin wrote some of his most important works, including *The Conquest of Bread* (1892) and *Mutual Aid* (1902). In *Mutual Aid,* he combined scientific and political theories, concluding that mutual aid, or cooperation, was most essential to the development of both animal and human societies. This concept contrasted with the "survival of the fittest" theories put forth by British biologist Charles Darwin because Kropotkin believed that the world was actually a "struggle between organisms and the environment." His theories on anarchist Communism envisioned a world without money or property. In his younger years, Kropotkin supported the use of violence, calling for "propaganda by deed" to create change.

CHAPTER 4

ANARCHISM FROM 1848 TO 1914

Anarchist theories continued to gain popularity as the nineteenth century progressed. As the writings of Proudhon, Marx, and Bakunin continued to find an audience, more people began to consider alternatives to modern society.

THE 1848 REVOLUTIONS

In 1848, political revolutions sprang up in countries across Europe, including France, Germany, and Italy. People began to fight to remove oppressive monarchies and governments. For more than fifty years, the gap between rich and poor continued to widen. Hoping for change also, business owners believed moving away from conservative monarchies would allow them to make more money. At the same time, many wealthy people grew fearful of how they would be treated by the working class after a successful revolution.

The success of the French Revolution inspired people in other European countries to rebel against the monarchies that ruled over them. The revolutions of 1848 put these ideas into action across the continent.

In France, citizens hoped a new type of representative government would replace the French monarchy. In Germany and Italy, small states under the control of monarchies began to embrace nationalism—the idea of a unified homeland. The revolution in France was successful. Rebels removed King Louis-Philippe (1793–1830) from his throne and elected Louis-Napoléon Bonaparte (1808–1873) as president. Outside of France, most of the revolutions failed. Armies remained loyal to their governments, which prevented many rebellions from growing. Some rulers became more oppressive, banning books and organizations with revolutionary ideas. Despite this punishment, the thirst for change still remained. In Italy and Austria, for example, people continued to fight to unify throughout the century. The revolutions of 1848 had a worldwide effect on political movements, inspiring the foundation of the IWA later that year.

THE PARIS COMMUNE

Four years after his election, Louis-Napoléon Bonaparte named himself Napoleon III, emperor of France. In 1870, the Second

Like the emperors of ancient Rome, Napoléon Bonaparte had a column with a statue of himself erected in Paris. The statue was toppled during the French Commune but rebuilt within five years.

French Empire declared war against Prussia (today part of Germany). In less than a year, Prussian forces had surrounded Paris, forcing France to surrender. Prussian troops remained in the capital as part of the terms of surrender. The citizen-based National Guard refused to disarm, however, and Paris soon separated itself from the national government. The Parisian rebels formed a new government on March 26, 1871: the Paris Commune.

The commune attempted some of the more radical goals of the French Revolution (1789). New policies were instituted that favored the working class, including shorter workdays. Separation of church and state was stressed. But the commune was short lived; on May 28, the French government invaded Paris and destroyed the commune. Large sections of Paris were burned to the ground by both sides, resulting in the deaths of over twenty thousand rebels. Despite the bloodshed, the events inspired anarchists around the world. The commune was one of the first left-wing revolutions, and it convinced many radicals that violence was a legitimate method to change a society. These ideas would continue to influence revolutionary movements into the twentieth century.

CROSS-ATLANTIC ANARCHISM

American workers were enthusiastic about labor unions as well. The Industrial Revolution had created the same poor working conditions for them as in Europe. Many felt forgotten and neglect-ed by their employers in place of profit. Anarchist newspapers like Chicago's the *Alarm* were instrumental in organizing workers to make their voices heard through protests, demonstrations, and strikes.

LABOR MOVEMENTS

Labor unions emerged in the mid-nineteenth century. They gave workers collective power to ensure fair wages, safe working conditions, and job security. Unions were originally formed to protect craft workers with specialized skills such as bricklaying or carpentry. If membership was large enough, craft unions could control the amount of skilled labor in the workforce. Later, industrial unions formed to protect workers who did not have the specific skills needed to join a craft union. Most employers opposed labor unions; to them, meeting workers' demands would cut too deeply into their profits.

Labor unions are responsible for the benefits modern workers enjoy today, including health care, the ability to negotiate with management, and the banning of child labor. The antiauthoritarian ideas of the IWA sparked the formation of labor unions throughout Europe and America.

Anarchist organizations supported workers' causes well into the twentieth century. Some anarchists hoped that labor unions would eventually rise and gain control of production and move to a more cooperative system. This idea was the beginning of anarcho-syndicalism.

IMMIGRATION AND ANARCHISM

According to the Library of Congress, more than fifteen million immigrants came to the United States between 1900 and 1915. In the previous century, it took forty years for the same number to enter America. This new wave of immigrants was different from previous ones. Most were Catholic and from eastern and southern Europe. They entered American life at the bottom

This 1886 drawing depicts the Haymarket Square Riot. Although the event turned a large segment of the public against labor unions, it also strengthened the workers' movement, leading to the institution of an eight-hour workday.

of the social hierarchy. Many took low-paying jobs that native speaking Americans would not perform. These new citizens faced prejudice and discrimination at every turn. Disappointed by the lack of opportunities in their new home, some turned to anarchism, hoping that a newer, fairer system could change their fortunes. Immigrants were vital to both the labor movement and the spread of anarchist philosophy.

THE HAYMARKET SQUARE RIOT (1886)

On May 4, 1886, thousands of workers met at Chicago's Haymarket Square to lobby for a reasonable request: an eight-hour workday. Many of them had been on strike for fairer treatment in the workplace. Rather than negotiate, many business owners hired nonunion workers to keep production moving. When some of these strikebreakers were threatened by striking workers, police stepped in.

A bomb thrown from the crowd killed an officer. The peaceful demonstration quickly turned into a full-scale riot. Police fired into the crowd, killing both fellow officers and protesters. In the violence that followed, eight people lost their lives and hundreds were injured from both sides.

Eight men were tried and sentenced to death for their role in the riots. Although the violence of the afternoon came from both sides, the general public sided with the police rather than the protesters. Police raided union headquarters, often without warrants, and destroyed union offices.

Since they supported the labor movement, anarchists also became targets of law enforcement. Fear of anarchist violence began to spread through Chicago and beyond. Despite the retaliation, the quest for an eight-hour workday continued, and the forty-hour work week became law in 1938. The incident in Haymarket Square and its aftermath echoed around the United States. It had a particularly deep influence on Emma Goldman, a young Lithuanian who had recently moved to New York City.

EMMA GOLDMAN (1869–1940)

After the tragedy at Haymarket Square, Emma Goldman threw herself into anarchist activism. She had only arrived in the United States the previous year. Seeing the difficulties that she and other

After her deportation to Russia in 1917, Emma Goldman did not return to the United States until 1934, for a three-month speaking tour. After her death, she was buried in Chicago.

new immigrants faced in both their birthplaces and America, she engaged in the struggle for freedom against a capitalist society. An atheist, Goldman saw the church as another organization that desired to control people and restrict their freedom.

Goldman supported the use of violence if it brought about meaningful change. Inspired by Peter Kropotkin's theory of "propaganda by the deed," she helped a fellow anarchist plan to assassinate a union-busting industrialist named Henry Clay Frick. The attempt failed, and Goldman's partner in the plot was imprisoned for more than two decades. Later in her life, Goldman would still support violence but primarily for self-defense. During the early 1900s, Goldman was jailed multiple times for "inciting to riot," or encouraging people to act out violently against the government.

Goldman was not only one of the most famous anarchists in America, she was also the nation's most notorious female anarchist. While feminists before her had focused on obtaining the right to vote (which came in 1920), Goldman favored full equality. She believed that women should not be viewed as only mothers and housekeepers, but as equal members of society with the same rights as men. Goldman also believed that discrimination against gender and sexuality was against anarchist principles. Goodman's ideas were the basis of this brand of anarcha-feminist thought. These views were not embraced by all; at one point Goldman was called "the most dangerous woman in America" by J. Edgar Hoover, the director of the Federal Bureau of Investigation (FBI). She was deported to the Soviet Union in 1919 for being an "anarchist alien."

CHAPTER 5

ANARCHISM BETWEEN WORLD WAR I AND WORLD WAR II

Calls for change in the anarchist community would continue through the early twentieth century. As the world continued to advance, the needs of the people seemed much more urgent than fifty years earlier. Anarchist theory would remain at the center of many of the era's most important and violent events.

A MOST VIOLENT CENTURY

In the late nineteenth century, the word "anarchy" was becoming synonymous with violence. In Russia, Czar Alexander II (1818–1881) was killed by a bomb thrown by a revolutionary group known as the People's Will.

In 1901, President William McKinley (1843–1901) was assassinated by an anarchist named Leon Czolgosz. After he was apprehended, Czolgosz claimed that he had been inspired by the writings of Emma Goldman. Believing that Goldman helped plan the murder, she was arrested but released a few

The June 29, 1914, edition of the *New York Times* reports the assassination of Archduke Ferdinand and his wife. The assassin, Gavrilo Princip, was ineligible for the death penalty because he was only nineteen years old when he carried out the crime.

weeks later. Czolgosz received the death penalty and was executed. Bombings and assassinations continued. Newspapers, law enforcement, and citizens fixated on the violence, but very few stopped to consider the conditions that led to it. Some had begun to realize that violence alone would not change the system. As Peter Kropotkin wrote in 1887: "A structure based on centuries of history cannot be destroyed with a few kilos of dynamite."

WORLD WAR I (1914–1918)

As workers and anarchists pressed for freedom, monarchies around the world continued to acquire new territory in Asia and Africa. These regions had untapped wealth and natural resources. The control of these regions led to a practice known as imperialism. Imperialism existed long before capitalism, but the Industrial Revolution enabled empires to reach further and faster than ever before, leading to competition between nations. These rivalries eventually resulted in armed conflict. Although it was not the only factor, imperialist behavior contributed to the start of World War I in 1914.

World War I began when a Serbian named Gravilo Princip shot and killed Archduke Franz Ferdinand of Austria-Hungary (today the separate nations of Austria and Hungary) and his wife, Sophie. Serbia was a part of the Austro-Hungarian empire, and many Serbs wanted freedom from their imperialist rulers. Princip attempted to do this by himself. Soon after, the empire declared war on Serbia. Russia supported Serbia and came to its aid, which led Germany to join forces with Austria-Hungary against them. Within a month, France and Great Britain joined Russia, and Europe was suddenly involved in one of the bloodiest wars in human history. The United States did not enter the war until 1917.

The war split the international anarchist community. The majority of anarchists were anti-imperialist, but some, like Kropotkin, supported victory over Germany and Austria-Hungary. To them, victory over an imperialist power would be a positive development. Along with other anarchist thinkers, he helped write the *Proclamation of the Sixteen* in 1916 to declare their position, which was only supported by a small portion of the anarchist community.

DEVOTED TO THE INTERESTS AND VOICING THE DEMANDS OF THE TRADE UNION MOVEMENT

Vol. XXVIII   APRIL, 1921   No.

THE CHALLENGE ACCEPTED

Labor Will Not Be Outlawed or Enslaved

By
Conference of Representatives of National Trade Unions
Washington, D. C., February 23-24, 1921

WE ASK the American people to give solemn consideration to this declaration. It is the pronouncement of a movement that is consecrated to the cause of freedom as Americans understand freedom. It is the message of men and women who will not desert the cause of freedom, no matter what the tide of the struggle.

The American labor movement in this crucial hour here lays before the people the full story and asks them to rally with labor to the defense of our imperilled institutions.

Labor speaks from no narrow or selfish point of view. It speaks from the standpoint of American citizenship. And the indictment it lays is an indictment of the enemies of freedom and progress.

American labor battling for the preservation of American democracy and American institutions today stands between two converging destructive forces.

Standing between two opposing forces, uncompromising toward both, the American trade union movement today finds itself and every American institution of freedom assailed and attacked by the conscienceless autocrats of industry and the followers of radical European fanaticism. If either of these wins, the doors of democratic freedom and opportunity can never be reopened in our time.

Though inspired by vastly different motives these two unrelenting forces work toward the destruction of the same ideals, each using the other as a tool

(280)

Some of labor unions' gains were achieved through cooperation. More than one hundred trade and craft unions endorsed *The Challenge Accepted,* a document that explained the goals of the labor movement.

THE RUSSIAN REVOLUTION

In Russia, Czar Nicholas II (1868–1918) had tightened his grip on citizens for two decades, fueling dissatisfaction with his reign. In 1905, he responded to worker strikes with armed soldiers.

The enormous casualties of World War I also troubled the Russian population. Over two million Russians died in the conflict and almost five million were wounded. Support for the czar eroded. A little more than a decade later, the Russian Revolution of 1917 began with a worker's strike. Unlike before, the czar's army protected the strikers and eventually fought against the czar. Nicholas stepped down from the throne a few days later.

The revolution was led by Vladimir Lenin (1870–1924) and Leon Trotsky (1879–1940). As the leaders of the Russian Social Democratic Labor Party (or Bolsheviks), they restructured almost every aspect of society. This revolution was not a socialist revolution. Instead, Russia moved to a Marxist government and took control of the means of production. Russia became the first Communist country in the world. After two years of civil war, the Bolsheviks took control of Russia in 1920 and renamed it the Union of Soviet Socialist Republics (USSR).

ПОД ЗНАМЕНЕМ ЛЕНИНА
– ВПЕРЕД К ПОБЕДЕ!

Propaganda posters like this one from 1941 were important to Communism in the Soviet Union. Books and publications that did not support the state were eliminated and replaced by information designed to control the working class.

Lenin's government used power to maintain control—it outlawed religion and used secret police to violently root out anti-Bolsheviks. Emma Goldman and other anarchists were critical of the revolution's aftermath. The revolution changed the structure of government, but neglected the values of freedom and equality that had driven it. In many anarchists' eyes, the Soviet Union had become what it had struggled against: the state.

AMERICAN REACTS

The Russian Revolution sent shockwaves around the world. Fears of a Bolshevik revolution on American soil led the government to crack down on labor activists and anarchists. New laws limited anarchist influences in society. During World War I, President Woodrow Wilson signed the Sedition Act of 1918 to make speaking out against the government, flag, or military illegal. The government was willing to enforce the law. Eugene V. Debs (1855–1926), a socialist and chairman of the International Workers of the World (also known as the Wobblies), spent ten years in prison after being convicted of violating the Sedition Act. The formation of the Communist Labor Party (CLP) in 1919 only intensified suspicion of groups that favored labor reform and anarchism.

This period became known as the First Red Scare. Between 1919 and 1920, violent attacks on labor unions increased, and some states went so far as to purge socialists from their legislatures. A. Mitchell Palmer, the attorney general of the United States, began a series of "Palmer Raids" intended to hunt down, arrest, and deport anarchists and members of the left wing. More than two hundred Russian immigrants suspected of loyalty to their homeland were deported. The FBI was also formed during these years.

THE SPANISH REVOLUTION

By 1930, Spain had one of the strongest anarchist communities in the world. The working class had begun to embrace anarchism as early as the 1860s. The works of Proudhon were very influential for peasants and workers in Spain. For them, the wealthy controlled property because of theft. Anarcho-syndicalist labor unions were a source of strength and protection for workers. In 1936, the leftist group Popular Front won a majority in the legislature. The party was made up of smaller anarchist and Communist organizations that were strengthened by this alliance. After the election, the new left-wing government named a socialist to serve as prime minister, and several anarchists were chosen for cabinet positions.

That year, General Francisco Franco attempted a coup against the elected government. This event marked the start of a three-year civil war, from 1936 to 1939. While anarchists, Communists, and the Soviet Union aided the official government, the governments in Germany and Italy supported Franco. Both Germany and Italy

During his nearly forty-year reign, General Franco, shown in this 1937 photo, ordered the deaths of thousands of Spanish citizens by the use of death squads.

were fascist—they believed in authoritarian governments that controlled all political and economic activity. Over thirty thousand citizens from countries that remained neutral volunteered for the Spanish international brigades to fight Franco. Within the country, tens of thousands of workers joined anarcho-syndicalist militias. Despite the resistance, Franco won the war with military aid from the fascist governments in Germany and Italy. He quickly installed a military dictatorship and named himself leader. Franco's reign lasted until 1975.

WORLD WAR II (1939–1945)

The financial penalties the Allied powers had placed on Germany after World War I led to an economic depression. Under Adolf Hitler, Germany rebuilt. Great Britain declared war on Germany after Germany invaded Poland and France in the late 1930s. The war soon spread to Europe, Asia, and Africa. The United States joined the battle from 1941 until the war ended in 1945. The Allied victory over the Axis nations of Germany, Italy, and Japan crippled international fascism and nationalist movements. Anarchists and revolutionary socialists hoped anti-capitalist revolutions would occur in countries that had been occupied during the war. Anti-imperialist ideas spread, leading to the liberation of American and European colonies in Asia and Africa. Although the balance of world power had shifted in favor of America after World War II, imperialism still existed. The Soviet Union and America spent much of the next fifty years struggling against each other to prevent the growth of both capitalism and Communism in other countries.

CHAPTER 6

ANARCHISM FROM 1945 TO TODAY

After a decline following World War II, interest in anarchism has begun to increase once more. From the World Trade Organization (WTO) protests in 1999 to Antifa, anarchist philosophy continues to influence some of the most important social movements of the twenty-first century.

THE NEW LEFT AND THE COUNTERCULTURE

The violence of the first half of the century had helped turn public opinion against anarchism and labor movements. Additionally, the Cold War between the USSR and the United States began to dominate American politics. Anarchist movements did not disappear, though. Anarchists continued to support workers' rights and revolutionary ideals. In the 1950s and 1960s, these values were upheld and promoted by the New Left. The New Left was not one specific group, instead the name applied to a group of left-wing anti-authoritarian thinkers and organizations. Many were influenced by earlier anarchist movements. The anarchist community also expanded its focus during these years, devoting attention to new issues, including the environment and civil rights.

The ideas of personal liberty and complete freedom were instrumental to the 1960s counterculture. Many anarchists were involved in protests against the Vietnam War (1954–1975). Vietnam had been colonized by France in the late 1880s. In 1954, the northern portion of Vietnam won its independence from France, dividing the country between Communist North Vietnam and socialist South Vietnam. Fearing a Communist takeover of the entire country, the United States entered the war in the 1960s. While many Americans supported battling Communism, others viewed the war in Vietnam as a return to America's imperialist past. Demonstrations often resulted in violence between protesters and police.

As working and living conditions deteriorated in America's inner cities, crime increased as well. In combating crime, police often used brutal methods to maintain order. Friction between them and the community caused riots and unrest in cities around the nation. Groups like the Black Panthers drew from anarchist and revolutionary theory to protect their communities from discrimination and police brutality.

PUNK ROCK

Rock music's rebellious attitude has often drawn supporters of anarchism. In 1970s England, a lack of employment opportunities caused many young people to express their frustration through a new type of music called punk rock. Punk rock (or "punk") is guitar-based rock and roll that addresses issues important to young people,

(continued on the next page)

(continued from the previous page)

including alienation, government policy, and social problems. Many punk bands have a "do-it-yourself," or DIY, spirit. Bands with like The Sex Pistols used anarchist imagery and songs ("Anarchy in the U.K.") to shock the public. As punk records began to sell, curiosity about these bands increased. While some groups played with the ideas and imagery of anarchism, others saw punk as a means to push for change and fight injustice.

Social problems concern many punk musicians and their fans. After the birth of punk rock, racist English neo-Nazis, known as skinheads for their shaved heads, would often recruit young people at shows. This situation led to the formation of the Anti-Fascist Action Network (AFA) in 1985. The AFA supported violence against fascist and racist groups, viewing them as immoral and unacceptable in society.

As in the anarchist community, punk rock exists in different forms. Anarcho-punk began in the 1970s and 1980s with bands like Crass, who advocated anarchism as a philosophy for life. Today, the influence of the original anarcho-punk movement can be felt in other types of punk.

THE ANTI-GLOBALIZATION MOVEMENT

Anarchist ideas regained popularity in the late 1990s. One of the greatest concerns was globalization. Opponents believed the opening of free trade by international organizations like the WTO had allowed the wealthy to exploit the people and resources of poorer countries. Anti-globalists thought that multinational corporations had become the face of a new type of imperialism, and union members, human rights groups, and environmentalists all supported the cause.

But some anarchists supported globalization. As Lucien van der Walt says in a 2001 *Northeastern Anarchist* article: "Many aspects of globalization ... should be welcomed by anarchists. The breaking down of closed national cultures, greater international contact, a consciousness of being a 'citizen of the world,' concern for developments halfway around the world ... are all positive developments."

On November 30, 1999, over forty thousand anarcho-syndicalists and other protesters met at a WTO conference in Seattle, Washington. While many protesters were peaceful, some took action, vandalizing public and private property.

THE WTO IS COMING TO SEATTLE

The World Trade Organization (WTO) is hosting its big Ministerial Summit in Seattle starting on November 29th. This meeting will set the course for multilateral trade negotiations on issues that impact all of us. These international trade rules affect the food we eat, the products we buy, the environment around us, and the work we do.

The WTO's record is a failure. While big business interests talk about the "benefits" of free trade, thousands of families have suffered through layoffs because plants are moving overseas where unsafe job conditions and low wages abound.

A secret WTO court has been deciding whether our laws and the laws of other countries are "illegal trade barriers" – including laws protecting our food safety, worker safety and the environment. So far, this WTO court has never upheld any public health, environment or safety regulation that has been challenged.

What Are You Going to Do About It?

Well-heeled special business interests have been pushing for this big globalized economy because it helps them make money, but the money never reaches ordinary people. Big business lobbyists have merely moved their back room deals from Washington, DC to Geneva, Switzerland.

Corporations have influence and access at the WTO, but ordinary citizens trying to protect democracy are shut out. One citizen has little chance against these global companies who care more about their profits than their workers or the environment. But, together we can make a difference.

The Time to Act is Now Democracy Needs Your Help Now More than Ever!

Join the BIG MARCH for Fair Trade

On Tuesday November 30th, thousands of people from all over the world will gather to protest the WTO's impact on working families and the environment. Join the global movement to show support for trade deals that put people before profits and hold common interests above special interests.

10 AM Citizens' Rally Memorial Stadium, Seattle Center

12:30 March on the WTO Convention Center

The world will be watching. Our governments need to serve the people when they negotiate these trade deals, not just the interests of corporate power. Join the thousands of activists who will press for a future which favors human rights, the environment, workers and their families and economic justice.

Mass protests were instrumental to the social movements of the late twentieth century. Many of these modern groups attempted to make an impact on a global scale by protesting multinational corporate policies that affected people worldwide.

Police confronted them, and riots soon followed. Although some anarchists did not support the violence of "The Battle of Seattle," they endorsed the media coverage of anti-globalization.

OCCUPY WALL STREET

Occupy Wall Street, or Occupy, was formed in 2011. Occupy members opposed globalization, the wage gap between rich and poor, and the growing power of corporations. Its slogan, "We are the 99%!" became known worldwide. Taking inspiration from anarchist philosophy, Occupy formed as a horizontal

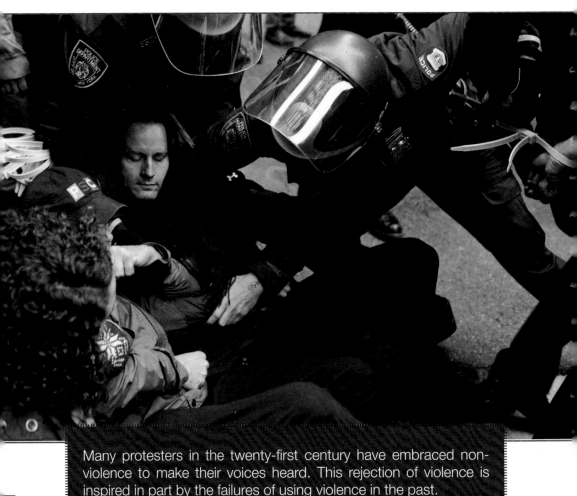

Many protesters in the twenty-first century have embraced non-violence to make their voices heard. This rejection of violence is inspired in part by the failures of using violence in the past.

organization with no leaders. Members also believed in a more equal redistribution of wealth. Occupy was also motivated by the Arab Spring, a wave of demonstrations and revolutions in Africa and the Middle East between 2010 and 2012. Some of Occupy's views were influenced by other organizations, such as Anonymous, an anticorporate hacktivist group that began in cyberspace.

Occupy set up camp in New York City's Zuccotti Park on September 17, 2011. Within a month, Occupy and organizations it influenced were demonstrating in more than eighty countries. Careful to distance themselves from the violent anarchist labor movements of the twentieth century, Occupy remained a nonviolent movement. Although there were some confrontations between protesters and police, no deaths were caused by these interactions. The New York Occupy camp was evacuated in November 2011.

ANTIFA

Antifa is a horizontal movement; the word is short for anti-fascist. Antifa groups have been fighting fascism around the world for years. A basic Antifa principle is "no platform for fascism."

Fascism did not die with the end of Nazism after World War II. In the twentieth century, nationalist and authoritarian groups operated on the fringes of society. In the twenty-first century, however, these groups have attracted more followers. Nationalism, sexism, and white supremacists have become the main target of Antifa groups. To Antifa, portions of the conservative "alt-right" movement are driven by those same nationalist impulses. In the words of Mark Bray, author of *Antifa: The Anti-Fascist Handbook*, Antifa groups "view self-defense as necessary in terms of defending communities against white supremacists. They also see this as preventative action. They look at the history of racism

Wars, famines, and natural disasters have led to a rise in refugees worldwide—this has also led to a rise in racism and nationalism. Both are targets of the anarchist community.

in Europe and say, 'we have to eradicate this problem before it gets any bigger, before it's too late.'"

Instead of resorting solely to violent methods, Antifa members employ a theory of "direct action" in combating these forces. Direct action can range from "outing," or exposing white supremacists, to employers, friends, and families, to disrupting the spread of hate speech and violence against women, immigrants, and minorities.

Although Antifa is often accused of being a tool of liberal politicians, the movement disagrees with the platforms of both Democrats and Republicans. The political left and right have both misunderstood the group, making the phrase "alt-left" a poor description of the movement.

In 2017, fights broke out between Antifa protesters and white nationalists at a white nationalist rally in Charlottesville, Virginia. Three deaths were blamed on the event, including those of two police troopers in a helicopter crash and a woman who died when a car plowed into a group of counterprotesters.

As concerns over globalization, climate change, and fascism continue to increase, people with diverse political affiliations agree on one thing: the current system of government is not working. Many in the anarchist community believe that representative government may not be able to solve society's problems. In his book *On Anarchism*, author Noam Chomsky says: "Power that isn't really justified by the will of the governed should be dismantled." The debate still continues on how to make that change a reality. The idea of taking a complex society apart and constructing something new is intimidating. Some may think anarchist goals are either too unrealistic or too violent, but the movement continues to attract people who desire the basic goals at the heart of anarchism—freedom and equality.

TIMELINE

4th Century BCE Aristotle writes *Politics*, an eight-volume work discussing types of government and the role politics should play in improving the lives of citizens.

1793 William Godwin publishes *Enquiry Concerning Political Justice*, which contains the foundations of anarchist philosophy.

1840 French philosopher Pierre-Joseph Proudhon publishes *What Is Property?: or, An Inquiry into the Principle of Right and of Government*.

1864 The International Workingmen's Association (IWA) is founded in London, England.

1882 Mikhail Bakunin's *God and the State* is published six years after his death.

1886 The Haymarket Square Riots claim the lives of eight Chicagoans.

1901 US president William McKinley is assassinated by Leon Czolgosz, an American anarchist.

1917 The Russian Revolution begins.

1917–1920 The First Red Scare includes increased surveillance of suspected anarchists and communists on American soil.

1918 Congress passes the Sedition Act to prevent citizens from writing or making speeches that are critical of the government and its institutions.

1919 Emma Goldman is deported from the United States to the Soviet Union.

1936   The Spanish Civil War begins.

1976   The Sex Pistols release the song "Anarchy in the U.K." on November 27.

1999   The "Battle in Seattle" causes millions of dollars in property damage.

September 17, 2011   The Occupy Wall Street movement begins a six-week encampment in New York City's Zuccotti Park.

2017   Antifascist demonstrators confront the "alt-right" in Charlottesville, Virginia.

"Anarchists Demand Strike to End War." *The New York Times,* May 19, 1917

Transcription Excerpt

Fellow-workers of the United States, why don't you do the same thing here that your brother-workers are doing in Russia? Why shouldn't the same 'wonderful and heartening things that have been happening in Russia' begin to happen right here? Are we workers of America going to let the workers and soldiers of Russia do the only wonderful and heartening things that are being done? President Wilson has said that America stands supremely for peace. And yet today the only place in Christendom where a single step is being taken toward peace is RUSSIA. War has come to a standstill in Russia. The Russian workers are seeking for peace in this world.

Workers of America, what are you going to do? It isn't enough for you to refuse to fight, to resist conscription, to denounce the Government. It is the business of American workers to do what their Russian brothers have done. The only enemies American workers have are in America, are the men who have taken the land, who are taking enormous profits from their toil, and who have them imprisoned or shot when they rebel—as has been done in West Virginia, in Colorado, in California, in Massachusetts, in a thousand places where the workers have rebelled against slavery and injustice.

Let the workers of the United States at once follow the "heartening" example of their Russian brothers and form a nation-wide "Council of Workers," which shall work hand in hand with "the Council of Workmen and Soldiers" in Russia against a war that cripples or kills millions of working people and enriches a few capitalists, and inaugurate here, as in Russia, the reign of freedom, justice and peace.

AFL (American Federation of Labor), The Challenge Accepted— *Labor Will Not Be Outlawed or Enslaved*, 1921.
Transcription Excerpt

The American labor movement in this crucial hour here lays before the people the full story and asks them to rally with labor to the defense of our imperiled institutions. Labor speaks from no narrow or selfish point of view. It speaks from the standpoint of American citizenship. And the indictment it lays is an indictment of the enemies of freedom and progress.

American labor battling for the preservation of American democracy and American institutions today stands between two converging destructive forces.

Standing between two opposing forces, uncompromising toward both, the American trade union movement today finds itself and every American institution of freedom assailed and attacked by the conscienceless autocrats of industry and the followers of radical European fanaticism. If either of these wins, the doors of democratic freedom and opportunity can never be reopened in our time.

Though inspired by vastly different motives, these two unrelenting forces work toward the destruction of the same ideals, each using the other as a tool in the struggle to overwhelm democracy and put an end to American progress, politically and industrially.

"Be Part of History: Join the Big March for Fair Trade, November 30th, Memorial Stadium."
Transcription Excerpt

Well-heeled special business interests have been pushing for this big globalized economy because it helps them make money, but the money never reaches ordinary people. Big business lobbyists have merely moved the back room deals from Washington DC to Geneva, Switzerland.

Corporations have influence and access at the WTO, but ordinary citizens are trying to protect democracy are shut out. One citizen has little chance against these global companies who care more about their profits than their workers or the environment. But together we can make a difference.

THE TIME TO ACT IS NOW.

GLOSSARY

ANARCHY A political theory that supports individual freedom from the state within leaderless societies or civil disorder caused by the absence of government.

AUTHORITY The ability to distribute justice and punishment.

CAPITALISM A system in which production and profit is controlled by individuals instead of the government.

CONSTITUTION The fundamental laws that govern a democracy.

DEMOCRACY A government with representatives that are elected by citizens.

ETHICS The rules of accepted behavior within a society.

HIERARCHY A system in which people or items are ranked.

MORALS An individual's personal beliefs about right and wrong behavior.

OBEDIENCE Following laws or rules developed by those who govern.

OLIGARCHY A government controlled by a small group, usually by birth or privilege.

OPPRESSIVE Controlling citizens of a society with strict physical or financial penalties.

PHILOSOPHY A system of ideas and beliefs about a subject.

POLITICS The ideas and policies needed to manage the government of a society.

REGIME A government.

SOCIETY A group of people who decide to live together under an agreed-upon structure.

STATE A country or nation organized under a government.

STRUCTURE The basic organization of any system.

UTILITARIANISM The idea that choices should be guided by the number of people who are happy as a result.

VOLUNTARY Using free will to make decisions.

Black Rose Anarchist Federation
PO Box 230685
Boston, MA 02123
(617) 419-0822
Email: boston@cblackrosefed.org
Website: http://www.blackrosefed.org
Facebook: @brnn.boston
Instagram: @blackrose_rosanegra
Twitter: @BRRN_Fed
This organization works for the benefit of the working class and
    local communities. Black Rose has fourteen local union
    locations in the United States including Boston, Chicago, Los
    Angeles, and New York City.

Center for Nonviolent Communication (CNVC)
9301 Indian School Road, NE
Suite 204
Albuquerque, NM 87112-2861
(505) 244-4041
Email: contact@cnvc.org
Website: http://www.cnvc.org
Facebook: @centerfornonviolentcommunication
This worldwide organization uses training and education to
    instruct people on how to resolve conflicts without violence.

Fellowship for Intentional Community (FIC)
23 Dancing Rabbit Lane
Rutledge, MO 63563-9757
(800) 462-8240

Email: support@iCdotOrg
Website: http://indymedia.org
Facebook: @FellowshipForIntentionalCommunity
Twitter: @icdotorg
This nonprofit supplies information and resources for both
    starting and spreading intentional communities in the United
    States and Canada.

Greenpeace Canada
33 Cecil Street
Toronto, ON M5T 1N1
Canada
(416) 597-8408
Website: http://www.greenpeace.org/canada/en/home
Facebook and Instagram: @greenpeace.canada
Twitter: @GreenpeaceCA
This international organization strives to protect the environment
    and spread the principles of nonviolence through social
    awareness and direct action.

Independent Media Center (Urbana-Champaign) (Indymedia)
202 South Broadway Avenue
Urbana, IL 61801
(217) 344-8820
Email: imc@ucimc.org
Website: http://indymedia.org
Facebook: @ucimc
Indymedia was founded in Seattle in 1999 as a collective of
    media outlets designed to free humanity. It has locations in
    the United States, Canada, and Europe.

Libertarian Party of Canada
372 Rideau Street, Suite 205

Ottawa, ON K1N 5Y8
Canada
(613) 288-9089
Website: http://libertarian.ca
Facebook and Twitter: @libertarianCDN
This political party works to "reduce the responsibilities and expense of government" and develop social harmony. This includes the support of individual freedom and the rejection of racism and sexism.

North American Anarchist Studies Network (NAASN)
Email: contact@naasn.org
Website: http://naasn.org
Facebook: @INAAnarchistStudiesN
NAASN is dedicated to the study and discussion of the history, future, and influence of anarchist theories. It organizes and hosts annual conferences in different North American cities.

American Anarchist. Dir. Charlie Siskel, Perf. William Powell, Charlie Siskel. El Segundo, CA: Gravitas Ventures, 2017.

Bray, Mark. *Translating Anarchy: The Anarchism of Occupy Wall Street*. Winchester, UK: Zero Books, 2013.

Curious George Brigade. *Anarchy in the Age of Dinosaurs*. Strangers in a Tangled Wilderness, 2012.

Danziger, Meryl. *Sing It! A Biography of Pete Seeger*. New York, NY: Seven Stories Press, 2016.

Golding, William. *Lord of the Flies*. New York, NY: Penguin, 2003.

Hinton, Kerry. *Sit-Ins and Nonviolent Protest for Racial Equality*. New York, NY: Rosen Publishing, 2018.

Kinna, Ruth. *Anarchism: A Beginner's Guide*. Oxford, UK: Oneworld Publications, 2012.

L'Engle, Madeline. *A Wrinkle in Time*. New York, NY: Farrar, Strauss and Giroux, 1962.

LeGuin, Ursula K. *The Dispossessed*. New York, NY: Avon Books, 1975.

Nagar, Innosanto. *A is for Activist*. New York, NY: Seven Stories Press, 2013.

Seven, John, and Jana Christy. *A Rule Is to Break: A Child's Guide To Anarchy*. San Francisco, CA: Manic D Press, 2012.

Uhl, Xina M., and Jesse Jarnow. *Socialism*. New York, NY: Rosen Publishing, 2019.

Worley, Peter. *The If Machine*. New York, NY: Continuum, 2011.

Zinn, Howard, and Rebecca Stefoff. *A Young People's History of the United States, Volume 2: Class Struggle to the War on Terror*. New York, NY: Seven Stories Press, 2007.

BIBLIOGRAPHY

Cahm, Caroline. *Kropotkin: And the Rise of Revolutionary Anarchism, 1872–1976*. Cambridge, UK: Cambridge University Press, 2002.

Carr, Edward Hallett. *Mikhail Bakunin*. New York, NY: Vintage Books, 1961.

Chomsky, Noam, and Barry Pateman, ed. *Chomsky on Anarchism*. Oakland, CA: AK Press, 2005.

Clasper, Ian. *The Day The Country Died: A History of Anarcho Punk 1980–1984*. London, UK: Cherry Red Books, 2008.

Cornell, Andrew. *Unruly Equality: U.S. Anarchism in the Twentieth Century*. Berkeley, CA: University of California Press, 2016.

Federal Bureau of Investigation. "Anarchist Extremism." November 16, 2010. archives.fbi.gov/archives/news /stories/2010/november/anarchist_111610/anarchist_111610.

Goldman, Emma. *Anarchism and Other Essays*. New York, NY: Mother Earth Publishing Association, 1911.

Gopnik, Adam. "The Fires of Paris." *New Yorker*, December 22, 2014. https://www.newyorker.com/magazine/2014/12/22 /fires-paris.

Gordon, Uri. *Anarchy Alive! Anti-Authoritarian Politics From Practice to Theory*. London, UK: Pluto Press, 2008.

Green, James. "The Haymarket Riot Remembered." *All Things Considered*. NPR, 2006. https://www.npr.org/templates /story/story.php?storyId=5369420.

Gueron, Daniel, ed., and Paul Sharkey, trans. *No Gods, No Masters: An Anthology of Anarchism*. Chico, CA: AK Press, 2005.

Jones, Jacqueline. "Perspective: 'Anarchist' Is Often Hurled as a Slur. But Can Anarchists Teach Us Something About Democracy?" *Washington Post*, January 11, 2018. https://

www.washingtonpost.com/news/made-by-history/wp/2018/01/11/anarchist-is-often-hurled-as-a-slur-but-can-anarchists-teach-us-something-about-democracy/?noredirect=on&utm_term=.ca788e16e68a

Kant, Immanuel, Robert Louden, ed., and Manfred Kuehn, ed. *Anthropology from a Pragmatic Point of View*. Cambridge, UK: Cambridge University Press, 2006.

May, Timothy. "The Crypto Anarchist Manifesto." November 22, 1992. Email. http://groups.csail.mit.edu/mac/classes/6.805/articles/crypto/cypherpunks/may-crypto-manifesto.html.

Milstein, Ciny. *Anarchy and Its Aspirations*. Chico, CA: AK Press, 2010.

Proudhon, Pierre-Joseph. *Property is Theft!: A Pierre-Joseph Proudhon Reader*. Chico, CA: AK Press, 2011.

Stein, Perry. "Anarchists and the Antifa: The History of Activists Trump Condemns as the 'Alt-Left'." *Washington Post*, August 16, 2017. https://www.washingtonpost.com/news/retropolis/wp/2017/08/16/a-history-of-the-alt-left-where-did-anarchists-and-the-antifa-come-from/?utm_term=.df19ba85e08e.

Stirner, Max, James J. Martin, ed., and Steven T. Byington, trans. *The Ego and Its Own: The Case of the Individual Against Authority*. Mineola, NY: Dover Publications, 2005.

Von Guttenberg, Mattheus. "Crypto-Anarchists and Crypto-anarchists." *Bitcoin*, September 29, 2014. https://bitcoinmagazine.com/articles/crypto-anarchists-cryptoanarchists-2-1412033787.

Zimmer, Keynon. *Immigrants Against the State: Yiddish and Italian Anarchism in America* (Working Class in American History). Champaign, IL: University of Illinois Press, 2015.

INDEX

ABOUT THE AUTHOR

Kerry Hinton has a strong interest in history and the intersection of technology and politics. This book allowed him to explore both ideas. He has written books for Rosen on subjects ranging from hackathons to 3D scanners to the trial of Sacco and Vanzetti. He has also been collecting punk rock records since 1985. He lives in Brooklyn, New York.

PHOTO CREDITS

Cover (pamphlet) Stuart Lutz/Gado/Archive Photos/Getty Images; cover (protestor in mask) Daryl L/Shutterstock.com; cover (police) Scott Olson/Getty Images; p. 5 George Frey /Getty Images; pp. 7, 28 Hulton Archive/Getty Images; p. 10 Tallandier/Bridgeman Images; pp. 14, 33 Heritage Images/Hulton Archive/Getty Images; p. 16 Stock Montage/Archive Photos /Getty Images; p. 17 Culture Club/Hulton Archive/Getty Images; p. 20 Everett Historical/Shutterstock.com; p. 22 Sovfoto /Universal Images Group/Getty Images; p. 24 Hulton Archive /Hulton Royals Collection/Getty Images; p. 27 A. DE GREGORIO /DeAgostini/Getty Images; p. 31 Chicago History Museum /Archive Photos/Getty Images; p. 36 Bettmann/Getty Images; p. 37 Public Domain; p. 38 Universal Images Group/Getty Images; p. 40 Photo12/Universal Images Group/Getty Images; p. 45 University of Washington Libraries, Special Collections, UW 39434; p. 46 Andrew Burton/Getty Images; p. 48 Pacific Press/LightRocket /Getty Images; chapter opener pages (world map silhouette) Vectorios2016/DigitalVision Vectors/Getty Images.

Design and Book Layout: Nicole Russo-Duca; Editor and Photo Researcher: Xina M. Uhl